Paint

CG Mclean Jr.

4-U-Nique
Publishing

Breaking the Status Quo, One Book at a Time.™

4-U-Nique Publishing
A Series of VLB/VBJ Enterprises, LLC

Painful Purpose
Copyright © 2019 by CG Mclean Jr. and 4-U-Nique Publishing

4-U-Nique Publishing books may be purchased for educational, business, or sales promotional use. For information, please email: info@4-U-Nique Publishing.com

First Edition

Cover Design By: 4-U-Nique Publishing

Library of Congress Cataloging-in-Publication Data

ISBN-13: 9781677244638

Introduction

We all are birthed with a purpose to fulfill. It is through the journey of life that our purpose is developed, molded, and shaped. The journey given is a trail of experiences called *the process*. The process progresses us to the position where we are prepared to take our platform for the building of the kingdom of God.

To whom much is given much is required. What if the verse was understood as follows; *much is required to whom much will be given.* That the required is a prerequisite to the given?

James 2-4*: consider it a sheer gift, friends, when tests and challenges come at you from all sides. You know that under pressure, your faith-life is forced into the open and shows its true colors. So don't try to get out of anything prematurely. Let it do its work so you become mature and well- developed, not deficient in anyway.*

This is a great time to stop and say what you are hear your heart say throughout this book; *"There is purpose, in your pain."*

Whatever the source of your *pain,* it is in this season of your life you can be rest assured that your pain has a designed purpose. Regardless of what it looks like, never mind what it feels like, and it definitely doesn't matter what others say it is if they are not speaking from the direction of the Holy Spirit.

There is purpose in your pain. Job felt pain and found purpose, Joseph experienced pain before his purpose took root. Our Lord and Savior Jesus Christ endured pain for the ultimate purpose.

What do any of those three have to do with you? Well I am glad you asked, if you are going through pain that seems unbearable for you, then I want to suggest and encourage you by saying you my friend are in good company. What may seem crushing; what may seem breaking; what may seem destroying, is only directing you to your *Painful Purpose?*

As we start to break down the what's behind the process I want you to hold on to, "*to whom, much is given much is required,*" James 1:2-4, and I want you to hold on to Matthew 16: 24-26, "*Then Jesus went to work on his disciples. Anyone who intends to come with me has to let me lead. You're not in the driver's seat; I am. Don't run from suffering; embrace it. Follow me and I'll show you how.*"

What we will learn throughout this time of study is that the pain, the process, and the promise are about God and for his people, and less about you and the picture you had about your life. The painful purpose is about developing you as a disciple of Jesus. Be encouraged my friend, "*All things work together for the good of them who love him." You have a painful purpose. Keep going, keep trusting, and keep believing. Hold on to your faith and you will see that God has been working in the background the whole time.* Now let's jump right in to it.

MUCH IS REQUIRED- THE PREREQUISITE

James 1:2-4, *consider it a sheer gift, friends, when tests and challenges come at you from all sides. You know that under pressure, your faith-life is forced into the open and shows its true colors. So don't try to get out of anything prematurely. Let it do its work so you become mature and well-developed, not deficient in any way.*

Table of Contents

Section 1
The Pain

Matthew 16:24-26 The Message (MSG) "Don't run from suffering; embrace it."

Chapter 1
Biblical Burning, Breaking, Betrayal and Beating

Burning

Gold is found in the midst of other rocks and materials. In order to get the Gold in position for refining, it has to be extracted from its original environment. There are four main ways that Gold can be taken from its current surroundings. Before we get off topic and into the marvelous processing of Gold, let's focus in on the *reason* of the removing of Gold.

Gold is removed from its surroundings because it's worth and value is too rich to stay in its current comfortable state. It's separated from its original state to become the focal point of enrichment. Plain and simple, gold is removed from gravel, silver, and other rocks because gold is too valuable, too precious, and it has a *higher demand*. To allow it to stay in a devaluing state would be wasteful.

11

The removal of gold from its surroundings is a discomforting necessity. The key in its removal is that the jeweler has an eye for what he is looking for and even in the midst of rubble, rocks, and other things the jeweler knows what gold looks like.

Once the jeweler identifies the gold as gold, they usually get excited because they know they have something they can work with. The jeweler separates the gold from the other things it's surrounded by and begins to prepare the gold for the refining stage.

The refining of Gold happens with burning.

What's the purpose? The purpose of refining gold is to burn any impurities left from the extraction stage. Once removed from the original surroundings gold still may have silver, granite, and other imperfections attached to it that would devalue its worth in the long run. The jeweler is wise enough to know what needs to be burned off for the purification of the Gold. The jeweler is wise enough to know that there is a process that gold must go through in order for it to get to its full value. Gold doesn't just go through a process; the value of the gold *grows through the burning* and the purpose isn't known until the **end of the process**.

Breaking

When we look at the story of Job, the devil wanted to test someone's faith to God and it was not anyone that the devil could find faithful enough. God asked the devil "have you tried Job?" The devil said well he only serves you because he has been given so much. God told the devil you can take everything you want from him just do not touch his body. The devil thought well great if I can take absolutely everything from him I can **break** his faith towards God.

Job was already a very wealthy man. He had a beautiful home, a beautiful wife, and great kids who appreciated and valued him. He had great friends that respected him. He had a great money source, as well as, a great relationship with God.

Job had an amazing life already set into place. If he had a strong relationship with God and did no wrong why would God allow the devil to break him down? Why Job?

The answer was at the end of the book but we won't highlight that right now. As stated before, Job seemingly had it all but everything he had built, everything that he thought was meant for him, and his bloodline was taken away. Job lost his source of income, his means of food, his children all died, and Job lost his wife. Through all of these loses its safe to say Job experienced a breaking but he didn't sin against God. He did *no wrong* in the eyes of the Lord. His faith was made strong and showed pure through the pain.

Betrayal

Joseph who was favored by his father had to ensure the pain of betrayal by his own brothers. Joseph received a dream from the Lord that he would one day rule over his brothers and family, and they would bow to him in need. That is one powerful dream. Joseph told his brothers and with them already being aware of their father's favoring of Joseph over them, they became overly jealous of Joseph.

Jealousy manifested itself into them coming up with a plan. Their plan was to extract Joseph from his family. The betrayal Joseph experienced from his brothers was them selling him into slavery. His brothers thought about killing him but worrying about the consequences that would probably come from killing him, they ended up selling him in hopes that they'd never have to see him again. It was their hopes that selling him into slavery would stop his dream from taking place.

That's only one instance of Joseph dealing with betrayal. After dealing with jealousy rooted betrayal from his 10 older brothers, he also experienced betrayal rooted in the lies and deceit of Potiphar's wife.

Potiphar's wife attempted to manipulate Joseph into sleeping with her. When he refused, she lied on Joseph and not only stated he slept with her, but she falsely accused him of raping her. It was because of these false accusations that Joseph was thrown into jail. Joseph had experienced betrayal from Potiphar's wife that was rooted in the disbelief of rejection. Undoubtedly, a beautiful woman who longed attention and affection of a younger man, she couldn't understand being rejected by a slave due to his loyalty to Potiphar.

While thrown into prison, Joseph exercised his gift of interpretation of dreams again. This time a few prisoners asked him what did their dreams mean. Joseph let them know that the first prisoner's dream meant he was going to be restored back into his former position in Pharaoh's palace. The prisoners was excited and overjoyed, Joseph asked him not to forget about him and to ask Pharaoh to have him released from prison.

This is where Joseph experienced a third type of betrayal and which was the betrayal of being forgotten. The prisoner received not only his interpretation which caused him to be overjoyed but he received his blessing of restoration from God. Once he received his blessing he forgot about the promise he made to Joseph.

Now before we get engulfed in the fascinating story of Joseph, let's stop and ask why? Why did Joseph have to go through so much betrayal when he received a dream of ruling and providing? Such experiences seem mighty painful for a dream filled with so much promise. It's a great question and one wouldn't truly understand the reason why until the end of the story.

Beating

The beating that Jesus took is a vivid picture that leaves lasting eyes of the hurt experienced by all who come to believe in the Lord, our Savior Jesus Christ.

"For God so loved the world that he gave his only begotten Son." Let's stop right there God loved us so much he gave of himself made into flesh his only begotten son. He gave of himself a son to a world who needed him to show us, his people, how to live selflessly and to give of himself as his service to mankind.

Here we have Jesus a man who has done no wrong. A man who performed miracle after miracle, and blessing after blessing. A man who formed a ministry that would change the world forever.

He traveled the land healing the sick and disabled, teaching the people of God, and showing all who would believe how to live. He turned water into wine, feeding

15

multitudes by performing the miracle of multiplication and showing the disciples how to be fishermen of men.

After doing all of these miraculous things why would he have to bare the cross and experience a beating like no other? To the human mind it makes no sense none at all! First off, Jesus doesn't even get a fair trial. His case isn't heard, he doesn't get to prove his case of living a life of no wrong doing. The people already had their mind up that he was going to bare the cross.

As if the weight of the cross was not enough, out of disobedience and disdain of **The Chosen One** they made him carry the cross. As he was carrying the cross to his own death he was whipped. They whipped him mercilessly. They whipped him like a common criminal. They whipped him like he did all the wrong in the world. They treated him like dirt; less of a human being. Repeatedly, he was gashed. Repeatedly, they struck him. As they hit him, they mocked him, laughed at him, and even spit on him.

They put thorns in his head until his skull started to bleed. They put nails in his hands so he couldn't fight back. They put nails in his feet. They talked about his position as the Son of God saying, *"is this your king?"* Is this you're chosen one? Look at him. They mocked, spat on, and beat Jesus to death. Why? Why though? If he did no wrong; if he was the only person in flesh to walk the earth to not sin; why Jesus Christ? Why did he have to go through such pain and agony? What's the point? What is the purpose?

Before we go into the *Powerful Purpose* of the pain Jesus had to ensure, let's first recognize a few things.

1. Even Jesus had to endure pain to fulfill the purpose God had for him. 2. While enduring the Pain Jesus asked God a few questions that may appall the average believer. Jesus asked God if there was any other way for the purpose to be fulfilled let it be taken. Then he says, *"God not mine will but your will be done."* He specifically said let this cup pass from me. I know it's mine I know I have to go through it yet if it's another way. However, he was strong enough to say, *not my will let your will be done.*

The second question Jesus asked God was, *"Father why have thou forsaken me?"* Whoa, but the Bible says *"God will never leave nor forsake you."* What type of pain did Jesus feel to ask God Almighty a question of that magnitude?

That's a powerful question to ask and before we get into answering it let's just stay at the vivid picture left in our hearts, minds, and spirits. Jesus experienced a beating like no other beating that is still being felt throughout the world. The reason why is at the end of the book.

I hear you saying it now all of these examples and stories are powerful and very touching but what does it have to do with you and everything you are going through? Yeah, gold has to go through **fire**. Yes, Job had to deal with losing everything; ok, so what Joseph had to deal with various versions of betrayal. No disrespect, but you see and get that Jesus had to deal with getting beat.

All of these things just may be true but what does it have to do with the pain you are dealing with? I'm glad you asked. Keep reading the answer is within the book.

Much is required- The Prerequisite

Chapter 2
Your Pain

Psalm 119:71 NIV "It was good for me to be afflicted so that I might learn your decrees."

I've come to a place in life where I have started realizing it doesn't matter how you are living; rather good, bad, or indifferent, life is going to happen to all of us. Meaning, the sun is going to come up on the good and evil. It is going to rain on the just and the unjust. That's just how God's love works.

Now I'm not saying this to excuse the way one may live in sin. I am saying it to say we all experience some good and some pain in life. Life's success isn't in just merely living through experiences but it comes from growing and learning to become better through everything we face in our life.

John Maxwell might say something like "sometimes you win, sometimes you learn." He may even urge you to "fail forward." Either way, it is important to know that while living this life, life is going to happen to you and no matter if it's your own undoing or someone else's. Pain will not only knock on your front door it will bust through it. The Question is when it does happen and when you do experience it, what is your mindset? How do you respond to it? Do you become bitter or do you become better?

When hearing such questions one may answer and say well, "it depends on what the pain is". Someone may say, "I don't know how I would respond until I am in it." Others may honestly be able to declare, "It doesn't matter what I have to go through, I know I can make it through with God with me." All of which may be good and true but getting through pain and growing through pain are two totally different things.

Let's take a look back at gold; we learned that gold is extracted from its original environment. It starts off being surrounded by things that tend to devalue it. The extraction of gold is a process of discomfort. After all, you are pulling it away from its normal surroundings.

If a jeweler knows the value of gold and knows that the worth of gold will increase when pulled out of its original environment. Those who are going through life and are being extracted from relationships, from family, from friends, and even communities, don't you know it's because God knows your value. Staying in your original environment devalues your worth.

I understand it is comfortable and it may feel natural to be in a relationship that is toxic. It may feel natural to be around family who understand your past. It may feel natural to have friends who accept you for who you are. It may feel natural for you to live in a community where you know everyone and how to get to and from without having to second guess or ask anyone for help.

As true as it may be that natural feeling, that level of comfort just may be devaluing to the real worth you have in and on your life. God has to extract you from your original surroundings in order to focus on refining you, so that you can reach your full potential in life.

If you feel alone, good you have been extracted for a purpose bigger than you. The ultimate jeweler sees your potential and true worth. He loves you too much to keep you in a devaluing state of being.

Extraction without refining is incomplete. A jeweler wouldn't be able to use unrefined gold in the same manner as purified gold that has been through the fire. When you are experiencing the process of extraction just know refining is going to take place. God is faithful to finish the work he has started. He will not leave you incomplete because incomplete is and would still be ineffective. The God I serve is far from ineffective.

Just as gold goes through the fire burning off impurities that came out attached to it; you will go through the fire burning off things that may still be attached to you. Extraction is one thing, refining is the true level up process because that's when the value and worth of Gold goes up. When experiencing the burning you to will rid yourself of original environment residue.

Think of the impurities you may have shaped from your past. Is lying, idolatry, adultery, lust, manipulating, stealing, insecurities, fear, anxiousness, covetousness, jealousy or guilt, shame, defeat? Trust and believe we all have impurities and they are all devaluing to the true worth and value we have in and on our lives. The fires that we face once separated from our comfort zone environment come so that we may learn to move, act, and respond differently to the things we face in life than we would have in our original environment.

The Burning is for your learning. Learn how to love yourself and others. Rather they treat you good or bad, learn how to love during the hard times. Learn to express gratitude and gratefulness even in the hard times in life. Develop the fruits of the spirit during a season where those you've been separated from would expect you to grow bitter, respond bitter, and develop a hard heart.

Be focused when you are in the furnace. It's in the furnace of trials and tribulations where you will become pure and fruitful, and your worth and value will grow.

Breaking Down

Job experienced a breaking like no other his faithfulness to God was tested when he lost everything. We learned how Job had everything one could want and to top it off he had a strong relationship with God. The question we walked away asking was, well then why did Job have to go through losing everything if he loved the Lord and did no wrong?

You may not have to experience the furnace because you have good fruit, but you may be more like Job than unrefined gold. You may have experienced loss at a major cost. Loss of finances, loss of a relationship, loss of a loved one, how about loss of peace, or loss of opportunities? After all, Job loss it all. Two things that remained were his faith and his friends, who had also experienced devastation. I'm not exactly sure the type of loss you have experienced but I know if you have experienced loss at a major cost the response you probably had is why? What is the purpose? What is the point? Or is there one? Let me be real clear here, it is ok to have those questions and it's nothing wrong with asking God genuinely what is going on here?

It's through the breaking and questioning that you can focus your attention on the source and not the resource. Job's testimony in the middle of experiencing the breaking was "The Lord gives and the Lord takes away." It's a safe bet to say Job wasn't saying this with a smile on his face. I can picture him frustrated and confused and you too may feel the same way. After all, Job did no wrong, yet and still he lost it all.

It was more than a game between God and the devil. It was more than God poking out his chest at a great servant that he knew wouldn't turn his back on him. God was able to show himself to Job and those in Job's influence, in ways that he would not had been able to if Job hadn't experienced loss at the levels he had experienced. God was able to show himself as The Source and a Restorer to the obedient and faithful. If you are able to stand firm in your faith; holding on to your relationship with God; remaining connected to the source of your strength when everything around you is breaking and falling apart, you too can experience restoration, healing, and transformation that only God can provide.

Facing Betrayal

You may be like Joseph and experiencing betrayal by brothers and sisters or other family members. It could be betrayal from people in an authoritative position, or from people you have helped and provided for time after time. The experience of betrayal is a real hurtful one because it hurts your ability to trust. It hurts your ability to love and it hurts your ability to give of yourself like no other.

How was Joseph able to face betrayal and get better? Joseph held on to the dream he received before experiencing the separate accounts of betrayal. God had told Joseph he would rule over his family. I'm sure he didn't know exactly, how? I am positive he didn't know how God would position him to fulfill his dream. He just knew that his dream would come to pass, come hell or high water, because he knew his dream came from the Lord.

There is something that God placed inside of you that we call *Purpose* and it's different from everyone else's. He also placed *Faith* inside of each and every one of us. The key to not losing any of these things while experiencing betrayal is to grow better and not bitter.

It's not about what is happening to you as much as it is about what is happening through you. It is very possible to go through storms of betrayal without allowing the storms of betrayal to go through you. When experiencing betrayal it is important to keep your focus on the Source of strength, the source of help. When you know that not only will he *Never Leave Nor Forsake You,* but that he truly will hold on to his promise that, Jeremiah 29: 11 "…I know what I'm doing. I have it all planned out—plans to take care of you, not abandon you, plans to give you the future you hope for."

Enduring the Beating

As horrid as it may be revisiting the crucifixion of Jesus, it is one event that allows us to see the depths of God's love for us. While we won't compare the beating of Christ to the beating we face in life, we will connect the pains that we all experience with beatings and see if we can draw out a good reasoning for the pain we face.

Jesus already knew what was to come. It was in this moment that Jesus started to sweat. He experienced a level off stress and agony that he started to bleed. This high level of stress and anxiety actually caused Jesus to sweat blood which is known as **Hematidrosis**. He felt the agony so much so that even Jesus asked God, *"if there is anyway this cup can pass from me…"*

There may be things you are facing that are causing a high level of stress or anxiety. It can be bills; your house may be in foreclosure and you could be facing homelessness. It could be failing health where it seems all of a sudden your health is deteriorating and you seem to be dying. It could be a failing marriage, where you and your spouse are at the very brinks of a divorce and you want to work it out and they have made up their mind that they are done. It may even be family members not wanting anything to do with you, even though you are ready to forgive and build a more meaningful relationship.

Maybe what you are preparing to face isn't listed. It still doesn't minimize the agony, anxiety, and stress you are experiencing. This type of pain is beyond you. It's bigger than you, yet it fills you in indescribable ways. Trust me I truly understand. Now is a good time to stop and say I Love You, and God Loves You More.

Let's turn our focus on how Jesus responded in the time of his deepest despair. Jesus knew he was going to be beaten to the point where he would be disfigured beyond recognition. In the garden of Gethsemane he prayed, while his prayer started off as *"please if it is anyway let this cup pass,"* it ended with a resounding, *"Yet, Not My Will, But Your Will Be Done."*

Even though Jesus knew what had to be done he felt such anxiety that if it were any other way for things to go he definitely wouldn't have mind exploring them. However, he was disciplined enough to know that God's will and way was what was absolutely best. It was best for him and everyone else because, there was *purpose in his pain.*

Some things we are faced with we may want to end in a different way. We want to explore different methods and outcomes. It is on us to be **disciplined** knowing we aren't in the driver seat but God is in control. We can say, **"*Lord Have Your Way, Let Your Will Be Done.*"** We have to trust that our **Sovereign God Knows What's Best For Us**.

We may not want to be homeless. We may not want to be sick. We may not want to be shunned from our family. We may not want to face prison time. We may not want to get a divorce and we may not want to lose a child.

26

There is a lot that we can come up against in this life that we may not understand or grasp the reasoning for facing such adversity.

It can beat up against us and every strike is a whipping slash and the devil is asking, *"And you serve a God who will allow this? You serve a king that makes you go through this?"* Now we are to a point the pain of the beating has us beyond recognition.

Well if you serve A God who is perfect, knows all, and is **All-Powerful** then why does he allow these things to happen to you? Jesus took a beating like no other. Jesus was hung on a cross with thorns on his head. He was laughed at, whipped and even spat on. "He was able to say, *"forgive them father for they know not what they do."*

When you are faced with people questioning God based off of the things that you are going through, or when you get to the point where you are questioning God because of the beatings of life you're faced with, it's imperative that you remember who your father is. It's easier said than done because even Jesus said, *"father why have thou forsaken thee."* Some may see this and say Jesus forgot who he was. When you reach the peak of your pain and the height of your sorrow. When your life has you disfigured, remember you can always take a deeper lesson from Jesus and **cry out to the Lord**. He hears you. His ear is inclined to your prayers. Remember, "The Prayers of the Righteous Availeth Much."

Chapter 3
The Summary

There is a higher reasoning to your pain then you can begin to fathom. Sometimes it doesn't even begin to make sense because you are in the midst of it, and in the middle of pain all you feel is hurt and agony. If pain was avoidable in life, all of us would probably do without it. However, we as believers are told not to avoid pain but to embrace it. In fact, we are told to count it all joy. Running away from pain or pressure will have us running away from growth and development; ultimately running away from God.

If you're fighting for your marriage fight like your life depends on it. If you are fighting to get relationships with your family right, I know it hurts but keep on trying to make it better. If you are fighting to stay alive and have better health, keep fighting. If you are fighting for your spiritual life while having prison time over your head, don't give up. Don't ever give in. Maybe you are reading this and you're fighting the pain of a losing a child or a loved one, **keep fighting** to get in the presence of God.

The embracing of the pain you feel to keep fighting even when you feel the burning, the breaking, the betrayal, and the beating life comes your way with can be described as the leaning on, depending on, and trusting God. It's that which will carry you through so much so that not only will you *go through pain but you will grow through the pain*.

Now that you understand that there is purpose in your pain. Hopefully it gives you the ability to trust the processor and helps you to work the process, which will have a positive effect on the outcome of your life.

Much is required- The Prerequisite

James 1: 2-4 *"consider it a sheer gift, friends, when tests and challenges come at you from all sides. You know that under pressure, your faith-life is forced into the open and shows its true colors. So don't try to get out of anything prematurely. Let it do its work so you become mature and well-developed, not deficient in any way."*

Section 2
Trust the Processor.

Proverbs 3:5-6 *"Trust God from the bottom of your heart; Don't try to figure out everything on your own. Listen for God's voice in everything you do, everywhere you go; He's the one who will keep you on track. Don't assume that you know it all. Run to God!"*

Chapter 4
All Seeing, All Knowing, All Powerful

All Seeing

One of the most fascinating animals in my opinion is eagles. Eagles' wings are amazing. The way eagles learn how to fly is jaw dropping. The way they fly in packs and stay together reminds me of team work. They literally fly in a circle to gain height with minimal work.

The most fascinating thing about an eagle is its **vision**. The eagle has some of the best vision in the animal kingdom. Some scientific people who do a lot of studying and a lot of research, mixed with mathematical equations have come to the conclusion that an eagle's vision is 4 to 8 times better than the vision of humans. That in of itself is amazing don't you think?

If we were eagles we could be on the roof of a 10 to 12 story building and be able to see an ant crawling in the grass. Not only would we see the ant but we would be able to tell the details of the ant. That is how impressive an eagle's vision is especially with things in their direct line of vision. They can see colors so bright and rich in detail that if we had their vision it would truly be amazing. The retinas of an eagle are coated more densely than humans with cells that detect lights. They are called cones which enables them a higher ability to resolve details and higher pixel density. Also eagles have a deeper fovea. Their fovea can detect lights from the center of their visual field because of their cone-rich structure in the back of their eyes. The convex pit allows for their eyes the extra magnifying ability in the center of their view.

An Eagles Focal View Is Undeniably Amazing.

To quote livingvisioncenter.com, "Visual acuity is the eye's ability to separate details of an object without any blur. The normal or a 'good' vision for a human is 20/20. Eagles, however, have retinas with cones and have a much deeper fovea—a cone-rich structure in the back of the eye. These give them a visual acuity of an impressive 20/5, or 20/4 which allows them to hunt even the tiny prey from hundreds of feet up in the air."

What makes this so amazing is that no matter how high or far away the eagle is from the ground its sight is still set on its prey. The eagle can fly to heights above surroundings and still see and know everything that is going on in its environment to survive and to execute its plan almost flawlessly.

The eagles make up, its build, and structure allows it to see the way no other animal can. It is built to be able to see the details of its prey even when at elevated heights. The eagle is an animal whose vision is one in the details.

I also want to be able to make a point to highlight that it's not just the straight line vision of an eagle that makes their vision better than humans. They also have superior peripheral vision as well. The eagle can see 340 degrees around them. Their vision is one of the best for all birds. To help focus on near and far objects not only their lens but their actual cornea can change shape. To further blow your mind, eagles it can see all of these angles with clarity while flying without even turning its head.

Humans have very good vision. In fact, it is naturally our strongest sense; however the eagle has stronger vision than we do. While the eagle has great vision compared to other birds and animals, their vision if of limitations. The eagle cannot see 360 degrees around their head, and an eagle cannot see where they are not located. Their vision is limited to their surroundings. Since they are not everywhere at all times they cannot see everything in real time.

If the eagle is amazing and their built in vision can get you excited and overly fascinated, then what do you think of the vision of the Lord? The same Lord that created the eagle created you. Ponder on that a minute as you try and wrap your mind around the amazing vision of an eagle.

All Knowing

Boris Sidis proclaimed to have the best child rearing methods. He touted those methods around and the proof was in the pudding. He raised his son who is known to be the smartest child prodigy ever. William James Sidis,

Boris's son had an IQ measured to be 50 to 100 points higher than Albert Einstein. By the age of 2 he was reading the newspaper. At the ripe age of 6, yes 6, he spoke 8 different languages fluently.

Think about that, at the age of 6 knowing 8 different languages? All I wanted to do at the age of 6 was watch, "Teenage Mutant Ninja Turtles" and eat fruit loops. William James Sidis knew by the age of 11 entered into Harvard University. Yes, you read that right, Harvard University at the age of 11.

What is even more impressive is that after getting first turned down by Harvard at the age of 9yrs old. It was between 9 and 10 years of age, that he wrote 4 books. He took rejection and kept learning, kept building his knowledge base. His mother and father continued to cultivate an atmosphere of knowledge and learning. As their son continued to grow in his knowledge they paraded him around with pride. It was their belief well before he was born, that one could create a genius. Their son's success was their evidence that they were right, but at what expense.

After going on to lead lecture halls and learning over 40 languages the once child prodigy grew to hate the spotlight. He became an introverted person who didn't like fame or crowds. A smart, "know it all", kind of guy, who ran from fame, notoriety, and fell into obscurity. Dumbing down his own knowledge because he didn't want to be known. His idea of a perfect life was seeking knowledge while staying to himself.

His parents engineered his "genius", setting an atmosphere of nurturing William James' curiosity. They fed him knowledge and taught him how to learn. It was the feeding of his curiosity that grew his hunger for knowledge. However, he never could completely fill his appetite.

As astonishing as the gathered knowledge of William James Sidis is to read about and come to know, you are quickly reminded of his human limits as you read about his later years. He struggled to come to grips with other areas and aspects of his life. He died alone from a stroke in his apartment.

The thing about William James Sidis is that he may have been one of the smartest most knowledgeable human beings to live, his knowledge was limited. He struggled with coming to know himself and the purpose and use of the knowledge he had.

William had the uncanny ability to gather and obtain information unlike the average human. His hunger and thirst for knowledge was second to none. However, while he mastered the ability to acquire information he didn't know how to use what he came to know for the betterment of anything. Not even himself.

If his story has begun to fascinate you do more research. You will go on to find out that he had real struggles with knowing not only what to do with the knowledge he gained but how to handle himself and help others. He would go on to write books but couldn't effectively convey the knowledge he had in a way others could understand. His wealth of knowledge, more or less made him less relatable to others. He comfortably became an introvert and staying secluded and to himself was his comfort zone. For someone who had experienced the spotlight for his accumulation of knowledge and with being labeled as a child genius. His hunger for knowledge never left but his desire for success and his want to connect with other people and his life story ends ambiguously.

God Almighty has infinite knowledge that surpasses William James, Boris, and Sarah Sidis. God doesn't operate out of theory and experimental behavior as did Boris and Sarah. God created music, relationships, and the like of things William James ran from. In fact, God created the things that William enjoyed learning and the things Boris and Sarah Sidis liked to experiment on their son with. At the end of the day, God created them too. What it boils down to is yes, this family had a wealth of knowledge yet their knowledge is limited. God of the universe and all there within has infinite knowledge.

Perplexing Power

First measurement of **power** is the rate that electricity is being used in a given moment. They describe it by using the term watts. Osaka University in Japan; In the year 2015, Osaka University lays claim of doing the unthinkable, they fired the most powerful laser ever. They fired a laser that gave off a 2 petawatt pulse, which is equivalent to 2 quadrillion watts. Yes, 2 quadrillion. I don't know about you but I never even heard of quadrillion. I don't know how long you have to count to reach 1 quadrillion, yet alone two.

That's beyond insane to me. It's perplexing to say the least. The concentrated energy through the one beam was 1000 times the world consumption of energy. That much energy in a picosecond is new territory amazing for me.

After researching the most powerful laser and researching the Osaka University team who were able to tackle such an amazing feat. I had to briefly research what a picosecond is. Come to find out a picosecond is one trillionth of a second. The only thing known on earth that can move at that speed is light. The speed of light is a term based on the fact that nothing can move faster than light.

Back to the Osaka University research team. They needed very little energy input to create such power. The energy it took was of only a few hundred joules, which for comparison purposes are equal to running a microwave.

This magnificent laser was built with magnifying lenses and it spans over 300 ft. While not a lot of energy was needed, they used special glass lamps to boost the energy. Made up their Fast Ignition Experiments or also known as LFEX.

Of course building something of this magnitude to become the most powerful laser ever built took a lot of time. It took a lot of preparation, planning, and patience to get the record. It took months of trial and error to get to their goal on September 29 2015.

They made claims of planning to reach 10 petawatts. Asked what could lasers of that magnitude truly accomplish? One researcher bluntly stated "blow up things". Researchers worldwide want to be able to shoot things down with their lasers. Things like satellites could be shot down in an instant if it were figured out how to generate such power for a longer period of time.

The one thing that they are trying to figure out is a limit that God does not have placed on him. The laser is limited to time. God is not restricted or constricted by time. His power isn't based off of theory and experiments. It doesn't take God Almighty trial and error, and test runs for months in order for him to get things right.

He Has All Power In His Hands.

Much is required- The Prerequisite

Chapter 5
God is Bigger

Psalm 147:5 "He counts the stars and assigns each a name. Our Lord is great, with limitless strength; we'll never comprehend what he knows and does."

All Seeing

We talked about eagles and again they are cool and their vision is phenomenal. 340 degree vision can see ants 10 or even 12 stories high. Their vision is better than ours. 4 to 8 times better to be exact. Yes, all of this aforementioned is true. And if it is true for an eagle it's even truer for the God we serve.

God is omnipresent. Meaning he is everywhere. Not only is he everywhere; he sees everything and he is orchestrating everything.

Proverbs 15:3 tells us God sees everything, all evil and good. If you recall, we talked about Job and his experience. God saw what was happening to Job. He saw what the devil did to Job. He saw the devil trying to find someone to mess with. That's how he knew the devil with his limited vision hadn't tried messing with Job.

That doesn't just go for Job. The Lord also sees what you go through. He sees your pain, and he sees your agony. He sees your trouble, trials, and tribulations.

He sees everything that you go through. Nothing eludes his sight because he sees all. It is just like the watchful skilled eye of the jeweler who knows how to pick out gold in a place where it is surrounded by gravel, silver, and other devaluing things. The jeweler has a trained eye and he knows what he is looking for. So does God even the more.

Just as the jeweler knows what gold looks like. When God sees you he is aware of what needs be done to add value to you because he sees the environment you are in. He sees the impurities that are hounding you and slowing you down and devaluing you.

God also sees how he can use you in his kingdom. He has a vision for your life. He sees how he can use your past in the present to shape you for the future he has in store for you.

God sees what you have to go through. He sees the pain, he sees the trouble, and he sees the divorce process. He is watching the backstabbing you are enduring. He sees the financial struggle. He sees the chaos on your job. The trouble in your family and the struggle with your children he sees it all.

He is an all seeing God nothing eludes his sight he is an all seeing God.

He sees the future and the outcome now because his vision is not limited to time. His vision is not limited to circumstances. His vision is not limited to the past, present, or future. His vision knows no limits.

He sees it all in real moment because to God time is an illusion and **He Ain't Restricted To It**. I know it's not _proper_ English to say ain't. I just want to drive this message home, and make it clear as possible. His vision has no limits. Not space, nor time, nor grammar. **He see it all.**

In the time when pain becomes too much and I get confused and tired I go back to a song that helps me realize that God sees me and my struggle. When I start to struggle with my own insecurities and issues the song, _His Eye is On the Sparrow_, helps put God's omnipresence back into perspective. It goes as follows:

HIS EYE IS ON THE SPARROW

Why should I feel discouraged? Why should the shadows come?

Why should my heart feel lonely?

And long for heaven and home

When Jesus is my portion

A constant friend is he

His eye is on the sparrow

And I know he watches over me

His eye is on the sparrow

And I know he watches me.

While watching, viewing, and seeing all that you are doing, everything you are enduring and all that is to come, God has one question for you, will you invite him in?

All Knowing

It's one thing to see what's going on and not have the ability to do anything about it. It's another thing to see your struggles, your habits, and your life in its entirety the past present and the future. God not only sees what's going on, he knows. God knows what has happened, is happening and what's going to happen. God knows what is needed in your life and he knows what it takes to get you to where it is he wants you to go. Does it sound like a lot? Well, to you and me it may be a lot? To be honest for you and me it's too much to even understand.

For us to worry about all the knowing of God and all the fine details of our lives is too much. It will stifle our entire being. As the word says:

Proverbs 3:5-12 The Message (MSG)

"Trust God from the bottom of your heart; don't try to figure out everything on your own. Listen for God's voice in everything you do, everywhere you go and he's the one who will keep you on track. Don't assume that you know it all. Run to God! Run from evil!"

I know that we have seen that verse before; to be specific it was in chapter 2. But I want to drive home, *that his ways aren't our ways not his understanding aren't our understanding. If we acknowledge him he will direct our path.*

He has a life that he planned for you that he has already set and when we accept him for who he is which is God, Lord and Savior he starts to unveil what he knows to us as he longs to communicate with us as he desires for us to get to know him as he knows us.

Remember, William James Sidis? He accumulated and gathered a wealth of knowledge. He had a thirst for education and was coined a child genius. His IQ scores were off the charts. Ok, I wanted to refresh your memory about him, with all of that knowledge he didn't know what to do with it.

As he grew older he became an introvert not wanting to communicate. He didn't want to be known for his early childhood accomplishments. He didn't want attention so he hid in obscurity. Running from the spotlight; writing books under different names so no one would know it was him. He wrote books and some were horrible. The message he wanted to convey was unclear. He had a difficult time effectively communicating the knowledge he had to his readers.

Well God created the *knowledge*. The knowledge that God created is what we call *truth*. That's why he is all knowing. He doesn't have to accumulate knowledge and figure out how to contain and convey it.

He is the Creator, the Great I Am. He holds all knowledge in his hands.

He knows how to communicate in every way possible. Once, we become in tuned with him and in the right relationship with him we learn of various types of forms of communication that he has with those who come to know him. He has written the book of your life. He is success. He is love, and he is knowledge. He knows how to share it with you. His communication is tailor made just for you. He just wants you to invite him in?

All Powerful

As fast as light travels, as creative as the Osaka research team had to be to create the world's most powerful laser. I mean we are talking picoseconds and pettawatts. All some pretty awesome things no doubt. Our God is a **powerful** God who can change things in an instant.

Scientists measure power by taking energy and dividing it by time to get watts. Thank God you can't measure my God's energy for he never slumbers or sleeps. As it says in his word and we already know that he isn't constricted by time as his time is perfect. As a song writer once beautifully described, *he may not come when you want him but he will be there right on time.* The reason that he is always on time is because he ain't restricted by time.

How does one come up with God being an All-Powerful God? Let's take infinite energy and divide it by limitless and perfect timing. How do you describe that? Watts can't measure it? Numbers would come to an end? His power is unquantifiable, now that is awesome.

If you're in pain, he can pull you through. Experiencing trouble, he can pull you through. Facing storms of life, he can pull you through. A pile of mess, he can pull you through. In over your head, he can pull you through.

The same God that pulled Job out and gave him double for his trouble, can do the same for you. He ain't change. The same God that pulled Joseph through the trails of betrayals has the same ability to do the same for you. The same God who gave his Son to the world, so his Son could sacrifice his life. He then pulled his son up so he could defeat death and sit at the right hand of his throne. Yes, that God.

He is the same God, **yesterday, today,** and **forevermore**. He doesn't get tired. He doesn't run out of energy in a picosecond. His arms and reach go beyond 300 yards. Yes, he is a God who sits high and looks low. He is so powerful that he can reach way down if he has to. He can pick you up and pull you through.

He doesn't fatigue, he isn't tired. He speaks a word and creates things. He spoke a word and created the Heavens, the Earth, and all that dwells within. From the words he speaks. He is the Great I Am. So powerful! So strong! So mighty! The only way he can describe himself is to say I Am that I Am

There are a few songs that really capture God's power and the use of his power that really put into prospective of God being the processor. Once we get the true knowledge of the processor, it becomes mentally manageable to go through the process. One that captures the picture so well is:

"My God, is big, so strong, so mighty, yeah, My God's plans for me, and goes beyond my wildest dreams..." Then they go on to write, *"there's nothing my God cannot do."*

I want you to go back up and read that part of the song again out loud this time.

Yeah, that's an awesomely, amazing, All-Powerful God right there. Osaka University is impressive but they don't have nothing on The God we serve, and that emphasizes itself. The question is will you invite him in so he can flex his power in your life?

Chapter 6
The Summary

God is all seeing, all knowing and all powerful. Quite frankly, he can do all things but fail. Yes, he has a plan for you. Yes, he wants what's best for you. Yes, he can shape, mold, and mend you. He can do all of those things with ease.

He created the eagle. He created William James Sidis, and he created and constructed the Osaka University research team. In fact, to go deeper he gave the eagle vision. He gave William the hunger for knowledge and he gave the Osaka University research team the idea for the laser.

Let's go deeper he created you. He created your pain. He created those who betrayed you. He created those situations you are facing. He created everything that you are faced with. He created the words that you are reading and every page of this book. Everything that is good and everything that is pure comes from the lord.

I know you rolled your eyes, I can hear your laugh as I write this. What you are faced with ain't good and it ain't pure and he ain't the author of confusion, so something ain't adding up. Now focus on that.

1 Colossians 1:16 *"...For everything, absolutely everything, above and below, visible and invisible, rank after rank after rank of angels—everything got started in him and finds its purpose in him. He was there before any of it came into existence and holds it all together right up to this moment...."*

One more bible verse just for extra clarity; John 1:3-5. *"Everything was created through him nothing—not one thing!— Came into being without him. What came into existence was Life, and the Life was Light to live by. The Life-Light blazed out of the darkness; the darkness couldn't put it out."*

Yes, he created it all. Being that he has created it all, it is important to know, he is the processor. He sets the process into place for each one of us.

However, as powerful and mighty as he is, God has given us free will. We can either go through life on our own. Trying to figure things out; trying to make sense of it all. Searching for answers and continuously frustrating ourselves with things that are out of our control. Or we can invite God in our lives, relinquish control, and tell him, "God have your way.

At this point in the book we have reached a very, very important crossroad. No one can force you to do anything but I am strongly suggesting that this next portion of the book you take extremely serious. If you haven't yet, make the best most powerful decision ever by accepting and inviting the processor, God, our Lord and Savior into your life. Read this next section out loud.

The Decision Declaration (Salvation Prayer)

"God, I need you in my life and I trust you with my life. I am a sinner and I constantly fall short. I need your help to live a life of love. Loving you, loving me and loving my neighbors. God, I come wanting to be made new changing my mind, my heart, and my soul turning away from sin and chasing you. I believe Jesus Christ died for me was buried for me and rose for me. I invite him in my heart and I declare from this day forward to live the rest of my life for you. In, Jesus name. Amen."

Congratulation and welcome into the family. I am proud of you and I love you. I give you an air high five and a big air. Wow! That was a big decision and a life changing one. It won't make life perfect but it is my belief as a believer that it makes everything in life worth it to have God the Processor with you every step of the way. And to have your spot in the Kingdom of God secured. Listen stay with the processor. As another song writer said; "don't give up on God because he won't give up on you he's able."

For anyone who has been going through pain and is battling and facing situations bigger than you, say this prayer out loud. Notice, I said say it not read it. "God, I need you. You are intentional and I know all things work together for the good of those who love you. I love you and I need you to step in and take control over the situations I face. You said your strength is made perfect in my weakness. Lord, I'm weak. I invite you in and I give you all control. Have your way and let your will be done. In, Jesus name, I pray. Amen."

When you know and trust the processor, it's easy to go through the process with confidence. Place all your Faith, Hope, Trust, and Confidence in God and grow through the process with **Godfidence**.

Much is required- The Prerequisite

James 1: 2-4 *"Consider it a sheer gift, friends, when tests and challenges come at you from all sides. You know that under pressure, your faith-life is forced into the open and shows its true colors. So don't try to get out of anything prematurely. Let it do its work so you become mature and well-developed, not deficient in any way."*

Section 3
Complete the Process.

Chapter 7
The Cake, The Puzzle, The Race.

The Cake

America's number 1 dessert is cheesecake. Man, as I write this I am salivating at the mouth longing for my mother-in-law's cheesecake. Hey, Mama Raine. I mean picture cheesecake with real strawberry toppings. Oozing down the side. Sounds so good right now, doesn't it?

Ok, as good as that sounds I don't know the least bit about making cheesecake, so we will settle for another one of my favorites. A good homemade old fashioned pound cake.

Now I've had the pleasure of being mistaken for a baker. While I can cook and trust, while I'm not the top chef type cooker I can hold my own in the kitchen and on the grill. With all of that being said, I know that baking a cake has a very detailed process. One must adhere to this detailed process in order for the cake to come out just how it is supposed to.

First, I want you to close your eyes and imagine a homemade old fashioned pound cake. Yeah buddy, can't you just about taste it? Keep that picture in your mind as we dive in to the process of making the cake.

Ok, first thing is we must know exactly what is needed in order to make the pound cake that's called the ingredients. To make the pound cake just right, just the way you tasted it in your mouth, a few seconds ago we need the following:

One pound butter. Softened 3 cups sugar 6 large eggs 4 cups all-purpose flour 3/4 cup milk 1 teaspoon almond extract one teaspoon vanilla extract.

Once you have your ingredients there are some things that you can do that will stop your pound cake from being as good as it can be. Some of these things will hinder it from being baked. Let's get those out the way so we can get to the instructions. Ok, here a few general don't do's if you want a tasty successful pound cake. Don't use the wrong pan. Grease the pan. Don't use cold ingredients. Don't scoop flour from the bag. Measure the ingredients. Don't under or over beat the batter. Don't bake on the wrong rack. Don't bake by time only. Don't use boxed ingredients. Don't slice into a warm cake. Last but not least, don't make too much noise near the oven Ok, that's a myth but I had to throw it in there. Now, that they are out of the way let's get to the instructions.

Beat butter at medium speed with an electric mixer until it's creamy. The butter will become a lighter yellow color.

It will take 3 to 5 minutes, depending on the power of your mixer. Add sugar gradually, while beating at medium speed until light and fluffy. Now the butter will turn a fluffy white. Then as you continue, add eggs, 1 at a time. Beating just until the yellow yolk disappears.

I know some of you are thinking, "I didn't pick up this book to learn how to bake a cake and this is a lot to do with something that has nothing to do with anything." Listen to me; I truly understand, sometimes life is that way. When we are at a job that has nothing to do with what God has promised us. I know I'm not God but I'm going to ask that you trust me because I am going somewhere with this. Again close your eyes and truly picture a nice fresh out the oven pound cake. Think of how good that first bite would be. Now there are a few more steps so work with me.

Next step you want to add flour to the creamed mixture alternating with milk, beginning and ending with flour. Beat at low speed just until blended after each addition. The batter should smoothen with flour well incorporated. Stir gently with a rubber spatula. Stir in extracts.

We aren't done quite yet. Remember the picture of the cake and how it tastes. For some of you the picture of the cake helps to read through all of the steps. For others, it did work and isn't working anymore. Then there are others of you who are totally lost and frustrated. I get it I truly do. Whichever category you fall under, I urge you to continue reading.

The next steps of baking a pound cake is to, pour the mix into a greased and floured 10-inch tube pan. Use vegetable shortening or butter to grease the pan. Get every inch of the pan covered. Sprinkle a light coating of flour over the greased surface.

The next step would be to bake at 300° for 1 hour and 40 minutes or until a long wooden pick (a tooth pick look alike), is inserted in the center and comes out clean. Once that takes place you want to cool in the pan on a wire rack 10 to 15 minutes. Remove from pan, and cool completely on a wire rack.

I know your thoughts are, "how long is this going to take talking about cakes? Don't ask me to picture it one more time. Don't tell me how it will all make sense in the end and don't tell me to trust you." You are probably ready to put the book down all together or skip this section. Some of you just got back to this section of the book again, if we are being honest.

The reason I get it and understand because in today's microwave society, *process* has become a cuss word. We want things **instantly.** Long drawn out steps that are too detailed can frustrate us. I will tell you to imagine the cake; I will tell you to I get it again. I do urge you to trust me because in the end it will all make sense. Be patient, keep going, and complete this section of the book.

I hope you didn't prematurely bake a cake before reading the instructions all the way through because some of the chefs' secrets to this pound cake include preheating your oven to 300° before you begin. Also soften butter at room temperature for 30 minutes. Yes, you are at the end of the cake baking section wanting to make a pound cake so you can get some use out of having to read through every step and in your mind trying to figure out what this has to do with *A Painful Purpose.* You are probably annoyed with me, I tell you what, tell me life ain't a lot like having to read all of these instructions and manage your thoughts and feelings! Don't roll your eyes just *complete the process* chapter!

The Puzzle

John Spilsbury, ever heard of him? Probably not and that's cool. The origins of the puzzle are traced back to him. Yes, a long cake making recipe and now this is history lesson and whatever else is going to come about some puzzles. Keep Going; complete the process chapter in the book. Imagine that cake if you have to I don't know but keep reading don't stop just because you're irritated or aggravated. That's allowing your emotions to take over the commitment you made of starting and finishing this book.

Now where were we? Ok, that's right, John in 1767 created the first puzzle? He was a map making engraver and his jigsaw puzzle was a dissected map which proved to be a genius learning tool. One thing about puzzles that people have come to find out regarding the time it takes to complete is that if you double the pieces you quadruple the time it takes to complete any given puzzle. Hmm now that is poetic within itself the more intricate the puzzle, the more detailed the pieces of the puzzle the more pieces to the puzzle, the more time it takes. As a rule of thumb, on average it generally takes four times longer to piece together.

Regardless of how irritated and annoyed you may be to this point you have to admit that's a very interesting point. Not only interesting, but it sounds a lot like the process of life. You've been made this beautiful promise, seen a very specific detailed amazingly jaw dropping picture. Yet, you are stuck with a lot of pieces. You feel rushed by the pressure and reality of limited time to put it altogether.

The things that interest me most about puzzles also can be the cause of frustration once I'm committed to completing it. The thing that drives me to purchase the puzzle is the picture on the box. The picture on the box is what the finish product is supposed to look like. On the very flip side of that if you will are all the little small pieces on the inside of the box that have yet been put altogether. Every piece in the box has been cut out with amazing detail. Every piece has been individually painted with laser like focus on the big picture. Every piece in the box had been created to fit inside of other pieces to connect to get her making one beautiful picture.

Now tell me that doesn't sound *a lot like the process of life*. All of these small pieces of experiences and gifts placed inside of you are detailed seemingly for a bigger picture. Given to you before you were born, yet, all of those pieces have a connection to each other for that bigger picture to be reached.

Trust me, Keep Going! Keep Reading! Don't Quit! It Will Eventually all Make Sense.

When starting on a puzzle, its best that you have a plan and that you stick to the plan without getting frustrated or discouraged. Some people dump all the pieces and start looking at the box. Guessing what pieces go where. That would frustrate me. Others grab piece by piece and organize them based off of how the big picture on the box looked. Then they start putting them together. Some people start on the frame or the border of the puzzle;

whichever you prefer to call it. Others start at the center. Great thing about puzzles, there are many ways you can go about putting them together. Plan or no plan; the objective is to put every piece in the correct spot and complete the bigger picture. Now no matter how frustrating the puzzle may get, the objective is to complete the process of putting it all together for the bigger picture. Doesn't that sound a lot like life?

The Race

26.21 miles from start to finish; Woah! Yes, that's how long a marathon is. I don't know about you but for me that just sounds draining. It may seem crazy for me to say but it does sound draining, even for a walk-on collegiate track and field and cross country runner.

I loved running competitively because it taught me so many life lessons that I will never forget and that I find myself teaching every day. However, even as a distance runner for the local AAU track; mid distance runner for my high school team; or the slow very forgettable walk on at Norfolk State University, the one thing I never fully grew to love was practice. Why? Because, the work seemingly came without a reward.

Now back to the marathon. The rule of thumb on practicing for a marathon is based off 12 to 20 miles a week. That's the starting phase of training. However, the key to training for a marathon is finding a plan that suits you and your schedule. Being disciplined and consistent and sticking to it.

Most plans will have you training intensely for anywhere from 12 to about 18 weeks out to build up into your peak race shape. Now the plan is flexible and you don't want to think that the plan is permanent and if you miss a workout you will fail the marathon or that if you beast a workout you will beast the marathon. Training is training and one thing marathon runners know is that life happens rather, good, bad or indifferent things will happen and you will miss some workouts the key is not to miss all of them.

Sounds too simple to believe? I know you probably are saying, "Didn't you just say you can't even imagine running a marathon, now you are telling me about plans and workouts that you haven't experienced?" Ok, I hear you. And touché don't take my word for it by all means. However, you should listen to Mark Corgan about marathons. He would be considered a wise counsel. Here is what he has to say about training for a marathon.

"Your training is always in pencil. One workout doesn't make a marathon." Former American Olympic marathoner Mark Corgan says, "A meeting comes up on the day of a hard workout, it's not a big deal if you miss one workout. You just don't want to miss every single session."

Keeping that in mind, when a runner is training for a marathon, it's important that they keep track of how long they have been running, every practice and the pace that they have been running at. It's the tracking that allows them to know how well they are building up to the 26.21 miles, and what they need to do to consistently improve for the race.

The key about training for a marathon isn't how long you run, definitely not about how fast you are running, it's all about knowing what pace you are running. You have to set a pace that will allow you to finish the race. Experienced marathon runners practice running slow. I can hear you, so I'll repeat it. Yes, practice running slow.

That being said not all practices are slow closer to race day. You practice your race pace for a longer distance. On those days towards the end of your runs you intentionally pick the pace up to build your legs and lungs for the race.

Again, all training isn't the same. A runner prepares a plan for what they need most. A little nugget I'll leave you with in regards to training to run for a marathon is that you don't have to practice running 26.21 miles at a time, because when you get tired on race day the cheers from the crowd can pull you through the finish line if you don't quit.

A marathon? Wow, that's difficult to even think about. I know I didn't talk you into trying to run one. Well, maybe for you I did. I don't know that isn't my goal. My goal is to get you to see the process it takes to prepare to run a marathon. What does this have to do with your purpose and God? Glad you asked, for starters running a marathon is painful. You don't even have to run it, if you think about what it takes to run one long enough you will start to get tired. Also, the 26.21 mile race is a reminder of one of my favorite Bible verse.

Ecclesiastes 9:11 ERV *"I also saw other things in this life that were not fair. The fastest runner does not always win the race; the strongest soldier does not always win the battle; wise people don't always get the food; smart people don't always get the wealth; educated people don't always get the praise they deserve. When the time comes, bad things can happen to anyone!"*

In the Marathon of Life, I don't care how fast you run. It doesn't matter how smart of a race you run, as long as you keep running you will get tired. You will get thirsty. You will feel pain. The key to it all is to keep going. *Don't ever quit and endure until the end, giving the best you have with all that you have.*

Chapter 8
The Summary

No need to tell you God's preparation is more valuable than marathon training. As grueling as it may truly be, it would be a waste of breathe to reiterate how God is putting all the pieces of your life together and using all things for your good. He is using these pieces to complete one beautiful picture. It goes without saying, "Life is far from a piece of cake." It's a lot closer to a marathon than a cake walk.

The process God has for you is all about the details. The details of every moment, all of the good, all of the pain, all of the triumph, and all of the trials. Every single detail is used to shape you. He is the Potter and we are the clay. We are on the wheel of life and he is working on you. The process is his way of shaping you for his purpose. Now that you have a relationship with him you are in his hands. You can trust and believe that he is faithful to complete the great work he started in you.

You serve a God who knows every detail about you. Even down to the number of hairs you have on your head. If you watch carefully and pay attention to what he is doing and how he is doing it, you will catch the details.

Let's break down chapter 7 in great detail to see if you can unfold the process into greater meaning and tie it all in together for a great reasoning. Chapter 7 is the Cake, Puzzle, and Race chapter. They all break down individual pieces of seemingly separate things that have nothing to do with each other, or do they? Let's see. Now cake begins with the Letter C in this section were do's and don'ts of baking and specific detailed instructions on how to properly make a pound cake.

Depending on how well you follow instructions will determine how your cake tastes when it is done. Also, to add this section was intentionally long; however, like God, I asked that you imagine the finish product. I reminded you of the finish product throughout the detailed instructions. This was done intentionally to hold your focus throughout the section so you can complete the commitment. Regardless, of emotions and feelings you may have had.

Then there was the part about Puzzle pieces. In this section it was explained that the details of each individual piece of the puzzle and how each of the puzzle pieces connected to each other to make a bigger picture. I want you to hold on to the fact that the word puzzle begins with the letter P. We learned about the creator of the puzzle and some of his history.

We also talked about having a plan when putting a puzzle together. The picture shown on the box was the reason for buying the puzzle in the first place. Knowing that the picture made all the individually detailed pieces make sense.

You can try to take the puzzle pieces of life in your hands and try to put the puzzle together. Or you can hand them to God the creator with the history of making and putting puzzles together and let him show you how the puzzle is supposed to go. Question is, do you trust him to enough to give him the puzzle of your life?

R. Yes, the word Race starts with R and that was the final section of chapter 7. We talked about the marathon race and its grueling 26.21 mile distance. Yikes! We talked about the disciplined regiment it takes for marathon runners to properly prepare for such a race. I made mention of crowds pulling runners through with cheers and rather it comes by large groups or random individuals. In the race of life, God will place those who need to be around you around you to cheer you on.

Often when running the marathon if life we focus on people around us and try to see who is cheering us on. Who secretly hates on us, which is not all that important to tell you the truth. Just like the myth of too much noise by the oven will make your cake fall. The growing myth of having haters around you will cause you not to fulfill your purpose this can't be further from the truth.

God will prepare a table for you in the presence of your enemies. In the race of life, if you run from your haters you may also be running from the table he prepared for you. Focus on the race and your destination. The crowd will work itself out how God sees fit.

Tying all of this together, I told you to remember the C in Cake, the P in Puzzle, and the R in Race because those letters together form the acronym CPR. CPR is what the processor wants to do during the process. After having to stand the pain and getting to know God on a more intimate level he is performing CPR to give you a new life.

His process is breathing a fresh breathe inside of you. It revitalizes you for the purpose he designed inside of you. He is pumping a new mind, a new soul, and a new spirit all inside of you.

He is renewing you and making you whole. Some things may not make sense to you in the moment. You may not be able to see what your current job has to do with your calling. Or what the family pain has to do with your *"bigger"*, he showed you or how the numerous sleepless restless nights have anything to do with preparing you for your race. One thing I know is he wants to restore you. He wants to make you whole. He wants what is best for you and his CPR process is going to do just that. He has a GPS and as long as you trust the processor and complete the work of the process, it will all make sense. I leave you with a few Bible verses.

Romans 12:1-2 *"Don't become so well-adjusted to your culture that you fit into it without even thinking. Instead, fix your attention on God. You'll be changed from the inside out. Readily recognize what he wants from you, and quickly respond to it. Unlike the culture around you, always dragging you down to its level of immaturity, God brings the best out of you, develops well-formed maturity in you."*

Let me be totally honest, while there is a 26.21 mile count for what makes a marathon, there is no telling how long the process may be. You may get tired, weary, fatigued and all. You may feel like you want to give up I encourage you by saying **DON'T EVER GIVE UP, DON'T EVER GIVE IN**. I leave you with

Isaiah 40:3. *"He energizes those who get tired, gives fresh strength to dropouts. For even young people tire and drop out, young folk in their prime stumble and fall. But those who wait upon God get fresh strength. They spread their wings and soar like eagles, they run and don't get tired, they walk and don't lag behind."*

Chapter 9
Practical, Process, Practice.

In today's society the word process is a cuss word. Telling someone to be patient is like a slap in the face. We all know the saying "time is of an essence, I need what I need in a matter of seconds." Ok, you might not know the saying but you definitely understand the sentiment. The underlying message of I don't have time to waste or time to wait.

It's a microwave society that we live in where we want everything quick, fast, and instant. God isn't moved by our technology. He can and does use it but his ways are not our ways. I think it's important to practice things that we are far removed from to grasp a true understanding of what's being asked of us.

In this section I am urging you to truly practice patience. Working and completing the processes outlined in chapter 7. Practice the process by baking a pound cake.

Yes, bake 2 so you can bless someone with a cake and then you can also have your cake and eat it too. I think you deserve it because you got this far in the book.

Buy a puzzle any size you want and when you have time put it together. Sit down, challenge yourself and put the puzzle together. You may surprise yourself and have fun while doing it.

I know, I'm laughing thinking of the thoughts going through your mind as you get the puzzle. No, no, no, I'm not going to ask you to run a marathon because trust me at this moment I have no plans to myself. However, I am going to ask you to run, jog, or walk, whatever the Holy Spirit places on your heart. Go for however long he tells you to. One condition, let the Holy Spirit set that goal pace and distance and commit to it. Do it at least once. If you like it, continue it.

It's important not to cheat the process of life that God has laid out for you. It is what's going to help you become new for the purpose he birthed inside of you. Below is the recipe for the cake. I hope you enjoy the pound cake as much as I do. However, I challenge you not only to enjoy how it taste, have fun with the process of making it.

Ingredients: 1 pound butter, softened 3 cups sugar 6 large eggs 4 cups all-purpose flour 3/4 cup milk 1 teaspoon almond extract 1 teaspoon vanilla extract.

How to Make It

Step 1. Beat butter at medium speed with an electric mixer until creamy. (The butter will become a lighter yellow color; this is an important step, as the job of the mixer is to incorporate air into the butter so the cake will rise. It will take 1 to 7 minutes, depending on the power of your mixer). Gradually, add sugar, beating at medium speed until light and fluffy. (Again, the times will vary, and butter will turn to a fluffy white). Add eggs, 1 at a time, beating just until yellow yolk disappears.

Step 2. Add flour to creamed mixture alternately with milk, beginning and ending with flour. Beat at low speed just until blended after each addition. (The batter should be smooth and bits of flour should be well incorporated; to rid batter of lumps, stir gently with a rubber spatula). Stir in extract.

Step 3. Pour into a greased and floured 10-inch tube pan. (Use vegetable shortening or butter to grease the pan, getting every nook and cranny covered. Sprinkle a light coating of flour over the greased surface).

Step 4. Bake at 300° for 1 hour and 40 minutes or until a long wooden pick inserted in center comes out clean. Cool in pan on a wire rack 10 to 15 minutes. Remove from pan, and cool completely on a wire rack.

Step 5. Note: For testing purposes only, we used White Lily All-Purpose Flour.

Chef's Notes For the best results, preheat your oven to 300° before you begin. We also soften butter at room temperature for 30 minutes

Enjoy!

Much is Given- The Assignment

Section 4
The Purpose

Chapter 10
The Servant Leaders Task

The Master's Program

Gonzaga University has online courses for organizational leadership. This degree is one of a kind in today's world. I might also add it is very necessary and relevant. There is a focus and concentration in servant leadership. The school makes claim to be groundbreaking and very effective in this new innovative course. Leading the way it states the following on their website. "Grounded in the writings of Robert Greenleaf, Servant Leadership gives you the tools to grow as an individual and serve others, as you discover unique ways to transform your organization and community." They also make claim for promotions and raises for their students who complete the degree careers.

The catch to this degree, (if we can even call it a catch), is that it is a degree offered at the master's level. Even before getting to have the ability to obtain this degree there are other courses you must take and pass successfully. There are prerequisites that have to be met before you can be accepted to the program. However, once you meet those standards it is opportunity to grow strong and rich in terms of your leadership.

The courses that they have in place they claim will help you in a multitude of areas of your career in terms of leadership. Negotiations, leading change, conflict resolution, decision making and global solutions to name a few. Gaining knowledge in servant leadership would help someone exponentially on the job and home life. Strength and growing in these areas will help not only self, not only job, but community and potentially globally as well. It is Gonzaga's hopes that their new innovative courses become a front runner in leadership for today's society. It is their aim to not only offer these classes but to become a front runner in what it means to be a **Servant Leader.**

They make claims to a one of a kind new program for those who want to grow and develop in their careers. Their thought process is if they grow in leadership their ability for promotions and raises will also grow.

Studies have shown **Servant Leadership** has had a multiplying effect in the business world. It is this effect that helps people wants to come work, want to do better and want to perform at a high level constantly. **Servant Leadership** has had a major effect on the business worldwide.

Robert Greenleaf who is credited for coining the phrase *servant leader,* focused on highlighting the differences in philosophical behaviors in servant leaders and leaders who focus on money and power. Greenleaf was an organizational management leader at AT&T. While he gets credited for coining the phrase, others took his philosophy and started implementing it in businesses and forming their business models centered on this success breeding mentality.

What companies started to realize was that the more they implemented the servant leader mindset and model their customer service ratings approved. Customer satisfaction rose and their customers became more loyal to their business. When Greenleaf was able to start compiling quantitative proof of the positive impacts Servant Leadership had more companies started to take his theories, plans and programs serious.

The Servant Leader Qualities

There are characteristics that all servant leaders have. While these qualities may not all be of equal strength, strong servant leaders exemplify more consistent behavior in these areas than other types of leaders. Servant leaders have a strong awareness. They are empathetic. They are persuasive. They have a big-picture mindset. They are community builders, and believe in growth. Servant leaders know what is going on around them and it is the awareness of their employees and of their customers that allow them to keep their company in the know of what is going on and what is happening in the confines of their day to day work.

The mindset of a servant leader is to not only be aware of what's going on with employees or customers but truly care for each and every one they come in contact with.

Celebrating birthdays, knowing how their significant others are doing, and being there for those in need.

Awareness may end with a leaders surroundings but it starts with an awareness of self. The servant leader knows who they are. They are confident in their strengths, work on their areas of opportunity and that they are conscious of their influence and impact.

When you know your role and what qualifies you for your position, it leads to having the confidence and knowledge to know how your decision affects everyone around you. It gives the ability to truly capitalize on impactful decisions. It lends to consistent improvement of not only the leader but those within their direct report.

Empathy travels at the speed of light and builds trust. The one quality that allows businesses to grow exponentially is the ability to trust those in leadership. There is a quote I live by, "people don't care what you know until they know that you care." This quote is an absolute mindset shifter.

If you can grasp that when people know you care, they are open to feedback. They are open to change and they are open to the ideas given to them for improvement. It is the leader's job to remain on the level of the employees and the customers. It's the leader's job to help bridge the gaps between management to employees and employees to customers.

Empathy is the connector piece that says and shows, "hey I am no better than you and you are no worse than me. I understand you because I to have either been where you are or I can understand where you are coming from."

In the business world another quality that they feel servant leaders have or should have is the ability to be persuasive. Not being a dictatorial leader bossing people around or feeling that people should listen to you because you tell them to. No, but you should have the ability to convince people to follow your lead and direction.

Having the ability to help others to see why they should follow you starts with being able to paint a picture that is inclusive of everyone. Showing why they are a valuable and needed piece to a larger picture.

In the business sense the thought is you have to be able to get people to buy in to you as a person so they can follow your direction to where it is you want them to go.

The big picture mindset says that it's not just one thing, or one person, or one reason. That it is a combination or accumulation of many different factors that are connected that make the business run and allows it to be successful. The big picture vision quality in a servant leader allows them to communicate things that are beyond the moment's situation. They give everyone a vision of the future; the future of potential and possibilities. Big picture leaders understand the concept of little *i* big *WE*, weak me **STRONG US**.

These sayings are not to say they are smaller than anyone and or weaker than others. What it is really saying is, "as a leader, I will make myself small so we can be big together." It is saying, "I will be transparent and show my weaknesses so we all can prove to be strong together." The bigger picture mindset says, "the end result is more impactful as a whole than individuals and it takes a collective effort."

Business world servant leaders also have the characteristic of being community builders. Community builders see a need and meet a need. Paul Polman CEO of Unilever believes passionately that it is important to build a community in where employees and customers both can grow and thrive. As Polman has said, "You can put yourself to the purpose of others, and in doing so, you can be better off."

Polman's community building philosophy derives from knowing when you make others your purpose to improve. You get put into a better situation. You also benefit.

In the world of business the servant leader also keeps growth at the top of the priority list. Growth of the company is the big picture vision. Growth of their employees is the immediate goal. Growth of their products, services, and abilities is their most pressing need and growth of self is their constant work and effort. Once growth becomes the constant and consistent focal point of a group's effort, excellence is inevitable and becomes the cultural standard of everyone within the company. All of these characteristics point to something other than self for reasons larger than self. It's say it's about us but it starts with me.

Assignment Oriented

The assignment at hand is more important than the position that is held. Is the belief of those who are servant leaders in corporate America? What a leader is tasked with is in proportion to his gifts and abilities. They have what it takes to be successful in completing what needs to be done.

Where it was once ok to lead by fear tactics and whoever was the loudest and the sternest was the most respected and looked at as the best and most effective leader. Those days are long gone and a new wave of leadership beliefs is making waves in corporate America. That is where the servant leader comes into play. What researchers have found out is that more work is being done, more task are being completed and people are actually more effective with a leader who puts others first. While the task may not be top priority and positions are of less important, when you put people first, the objectives and assignments are completed more times than not.

Chapter 11
The Real Servant Leader

He started it.

While they may credit Greenleaf for the phrase, the mindset and the model came well before him and other leaders who have said they studied. The servant leader role was embodied and lived out by Jesus Christ. Christ didn't have to research it. He didn't have to come up with any theories or even have to drive a wedge between servant leadership and those who lead for power or monetary gain with books.

Jesus exemplified servant leadership with the way he lived his life. It wasn't a theory. It wasn't a plan. It wasn't an initiative started to turn around business. With Jesus it was a way of life.

Servant leadership is what he lived out and taught by example. As he was about his father's business, it's his genuineness and authenticity with being a servant leader that other marveled at. He knew who he was and he knew what he was tasked with doing. Which is evident by the words he spoke in the following scripture.

Mark 10:44-45... *"You've observed how godless rulers throw their weight around," he said, "and when people get a little power how quickly it goes to their heads. It's not going to be that way with you. Whoever wants to be great must become a servant. Whoever wants to be first among you must be your slave. That is what the Son of Man has done: He came to serve, not to be served—and then to give away his life in exchange for many who are held hostage."*

If this is what Jesus was tasked with when he ascended into heaven he also left us a task. Will you finish it?

Matthew 16:24 NIV "Then Jesus said to his disciples, Whoever wants to be my disciple must deny themselves and take up their cross and follow me."

Jesus Ministry was that of servant leadership. When he turned water into wine and he multiplied the fish and bread for the multitude. When he healed the blind and the lame; when he called Lazarus from the dead; when he went to the cross and gave his life; was buried; and rose on the third day they were all examples of servant leadership.

When he ascended into heaven he tasked us with the same assignment stating, In John 14:12-14 NIV 12 *"Very truly I tell you, whoever believes in me will do the works I have been doing, and they will do even greater things than these, because I am going to the Father. 13 And I will do whatever you ask in my name, so that the Father may be glorified in the Son. 14 You may ask me for anything in my name, and I will do it."*

We are able to do greater works than even him because as his disciples, we can petition through Jesus Christ for anything we want and for God's glory it will happen.

He went on to say he left us another advocate in the Holy Spirit to lead, guide, and direct us. It is through the Holy Spirit, we are able to receive the power to complete our task.

When we are faced with obstacles and situations we have to remember not only is the battle not ours, it's not about us either. Once we get that understanding we can find the **purpose in our pain** and **let our pain birth our purpose**.

If we are going to glorify the Lord with our lives than we must become his agents and share our stories of trial and triumph with others, so that they too can overcome what they are going through so to bring glory upon the Lord.

Why the pain? What's the purpose? Well for you to be a disciple of the Lord for someone else. What's your assignment? Glad you asked I will leave you with this scripture.

Matthew 28:18-20 NIV 18 *"Then Jesus came to them and said, "All authority in heaven and on earth has been given to me. 19 Therefore go and make disciples of all nations, baptizing them in the name of the Father and of the Son and of the Holy Spirit, 20 and teaching them to obey everything I have commanded you. And surely I am with you always, to the very end of the age."*

Go and Fulfill Your Assignment!

TheMotivation
My Pain

The reason why I wrote this book is because it was placed in my heart to share my testimony so here goes nothing...

Over a year ago, I made a terrible decision that hurt my wife to her core. From there our family has had to go through the process of separation and divorce. Over the year, as I began to get closer to God I have not only seen the error of my ways but I also had to experience the consequences of my decisions.

Those consequences include health issues, financial issues, and a great battle with anxiety and depression. I also had front row tickets to the pain of my wife whom I love greatly and have come to love ever so deeply, along with the pain of my handsome son and the hurt of my beautiful daughter. With that being said, the Lord has shown himself capable of providing strength, love, and peace beyond belief. He is truly a comforter in the time of distress.

I now know the power of forgiveness. I also have learned the ability and depths of God's love. He has instructed me and provided me with the ability to love without limitations, regardless of whom, what, or why. It is through the pain that I have found a deeper relationship with God our savior, encouragement, and through the encouragement I have been given the strength to complete the process that is laid out in front of me. I have become better and more focus on God and everything he is asking of me in this season of my life.

Now that I have fully invited him into my situation and given him full control, I say that my worry, anxiety, depression, and sorrow have lessened a great deal. I have learned through the process that not only giving God my situation but the emotions that are attached with the situation and just focus on him. He is unveiling his plans for my life with every step that I take with him. Through the process I know that I am positioning myself for a promotion that will elevate me for the purpose I was birthed with. In order for me to be filled for his purpose I have to be emptied from all of my impurities and selfish desires.

I wrote this book in the midst of my pain. It's been a 5 day journey of me writing this book through the leadership and guidance of the Holy Spirit and now leading up to this divorce hearing. I type this testimony in the court parking lot from my phone before walking in. I don't know what is to come but I do know God's love for me will never fail. It is his love that strengthens and encourages me when I feel empty. He has shown me that without a doubt. I encourage you by saying God loves you. There is **Purpose in Your Pain**. You have **A Painful Purpose. Amen!**

Regardless of how you feel, regardless of what you are going through **endure until the end. His word is still true and he still has a future for you. Be encouraged in the Lord, family**.

Scriptures

James 2-4 *"Consider it a sheer gift, friends, when tests and challenges come at you from all sides. You know that under pressure, your faith-life is forced into the open and shows its true colors. So don't try to get out of anything prematurely. Let it do its work so you become mature and well- developed, not deficient in any way."*

Matthew 16: 24-26 *"Then Jesus went to work on his disciples. "Anyone who intends to come with me has to let me lead. You're not in the driver's seat; I am. Don't run from suffering; embrace it. Follow me and I'll show you how."*

Psalm 119:71 NIV *"It was good for me to be afflicted so that I might learn your decrees."*

Jeremiah 29: 11 *"....I know what I'm doing. I have it all planned out—plans to take care of you, not abandon you, plans to give you the future you hope for."*

Proverbs 3:5-6 *"Trust God from the bottom of your heart; Don't try to figure out everything on your own. Listen for God's voice in everything you do, everywhere you go; He's the one who will keep you on track. Don't assume that you know it all. Run to God!"*

Psalm 147:5 *"He counts the stars and assigns each a name. Our Lord is great, with limitless strength; we'll never comprehend what he knows and does."*

Romans 12:1-2 *"Don't become so well-adjusted to your culture that you fit into it without even thinking. Instead, fix your attention on God. You'll be changed from the inside out. Readily recognize what he wants from you, and quickly respond to it. Unlike the culture around you, always dragging you down to its level of immaturity, God brings the best out of you, develops well-formed maturity in you."*

Isaiah 40:3. *"He energizes those who get tired, gives fresh strength to dropouts. For even young people tire and drop out, young folk in their prime stumble and fall. But those who wait upon God get fresh strength. They spread their wings and soar like eagles, They run and don't get tired, they walk and don't lag behind."*

Mark 10:44-45... *"You've observed how godless rulers throw their weight around," he said, "and when people get a little power how quickly it goes to their heads. It's not going to be that way with you. Whoever wants to be great must become a servant. Whoever wants to be first among you must be your slave. That is what the Son of Man has done: He came to serve, not to be served—and then to give away his life in exchange for many who are held hostage."*

Matthew 16:24 NIV *"Then Jesus said to his disciples, "Whoever wants to be my disciple must deny themselves and take up their cross and follow me."*

Matthew 28:18-20 NIV 18 *"Then Jesus came to them and said, "All authority in heaven and on earth has been given to me. 19 Therefore go and make disciples of all nations, baptizing them in the name of the Father and of the Son and of the Holy Spirit, 20 and teaching them to obey everything I have commanded you. And surely I am with you always, to the very end of the age."*

ABOUT THE AUTHOR

Community activist. High school Track and Field coach. Father. Disciple. CG Mclean Jr. is a man who lives by the scripture of Isaiah 40:13. "In life, I have experienced wins and lessons with both being blessings to get to know God on another level." As a minister in training, CG has been called by God to preach the word. As a vessel of God, CG uses his diverse talents to spread the Gospel.

CG heads a community initiative called Powerful Purpose. "I do a lot in the community because I believe the Church is the body of believers and our focus should be outside of the walls of the church building."

4-U-Nique Publishing

Read excerpts, get exclusive inside looks at exciting new titles and authors, find tour schedules and enter contests.

www.4-U-NiquePublishing.com

Need help publishing your masterpiece? We are happy to help.

Email us at info@4-U-NiquePublishing.com

Made in the USA
Columbia, SC
13 March 2021